Series 606A

Series 606 A

## STORIES IN THIS BOOK

A LADYBIRD 'EASY-READING' BOOK

# Stories about
# CHILDREN
# OF THE BIBLE

by HILDA I. ROSTRON

with illustrations by   CLIVE UPTTON

Publishers: Ladybird Books Ltd . Loughborough
© Ladybird Books Ltd (formerly Wills & Hepworth Ltd) 1962
*Printed in England*

# SAVING BABY MOSES

Aaron and Miriam and a baby boy lived with their father and mother near a river. Big sister Miriam loved to mind her little baby brother.

One day, the king said that all baby boys must be taken away from their homes. This made the family very unhappy indeed.

" God will help us to keep our baby safe," said mother.

7214 0060 4

"We will make a cradle-boat and hide baby in the reeds by the river."

So Miriam and her mother wove a cradle-boat of bul-rushes. It was cosy inside, and they painted the outside with tar to keep out the water.

Soon baby was safe and snug in his cradle-boat, hidden in the reeds. Sister Miriam kept watch near the river bank.

One day a princess, the daughter of the king, came to bathe in the river. She saw the cradle, and told her maid to fetch it. The baby woke up and cried.

The princess asked Miriam to find a nurse for the baby. Miriam ran for her mother.

"Will you nurse this baby for me? He is to be called, Moses," said the princess to the mother.

'Moses' means 'lifted out of the water.'

Mother had been told that the princess would look after Moses when he was older.

Mother and father were so glad that God had helped them to find a way of saving their baby, and of keeping him at home while he was so small.

When Moses grew up, God chose him to be a great leader and helper of His people.

# SAMUEL THE HELPER

Samuel was a happy little boy who went to help in God's House. It was called the Temple or Church.

His father and mother were glad that their son could be a helper.

The minister in the Temple was called Eli. He was an old man who needed a willing helper like Samuel.

There were many things to do in the Temple.

In the Temple there were lamps to clean and fill with oil. As Samuel grew bigger and stronger he was able to help Eli more. Samuel learned the time to open and close the Temple doors. Eli was glad Samuel could run messages for him.

Father and mother were so proud to see how well Samuel helped in God's House.

One night when Samuel was in bed, he heard a voice calling him. He jumped up and ran to Eli.

"Here I am. You called me."

"I did not call you. Go and lie down," said Eli.

Again Samuel heard a voice. He ran to Eli.

"Here I am. You *did* call me." Again Eli sent Samuel away. Then Samuel heard the voice for the third time. He ran and told Eli.

Then Eli told Samuel that it was God's voice speaking.

" Lie down again," said Eli, "and next time say, ' Speak, Lord, for Thy servant heareth'."

So Samuel went to bed and listened. Again he heard the voice call," Samuel! Samuel! "

Samuel sat up and replied as Eli had told him to do. And Samuel heard that God wanted him to be His special helper, too.

Samuel grew up to be a great judge and ruler of God's people.

# THE HELPFUL
## LITTLE MAID

There was once a girl who was taken from her home to live and work far away in another land. She went to be maid to the lady of a big house.

At first the little maid was home-sick, but the lady was very kind. Soon the girl felt happy in her new home.

The name of the lady's husband was Naaman (say it like this: Nay-a-man). He was very sad because he was ill, and no one could cure him.

The little maid loved her lady, and wanted to help her and her sick husband. She wished he could be made well and happy.

One day the little maid told the lady about Elisha. He was a good and holy man who lived in the girl's homeland.

God helped Elisha to cure those who were ill. So the lady spoke to her husband about Elisha.

Now the husband was a soldier in the king's army. He told the king about Elisha, who lived in the far away land.

" I will give you a letter and presents for the king of that land," said Naaman's king. " You must go there at once."

So away went Naaman to the homeland of the little maid.

Naaman asked the king for his help, but he said he could not cure Naaman.

Elisha heard about Naaman. He sent a message telling Naaman to wash seven times in the river Jordan, and God would heal him.

At first, Naaman did not want to obey. At last, he *did* obey Elisha, and God healed Naaman.

The lady and the little maid were so glad when Naaman came home, well and happy.

Together they thanked God.

# DAVID THE
## SHEPHERD BOY

David was a happy shepherd boy. He looked after his father's flock of sheep.

David had seven older brothers, but his father chose David, the youngest boy, to mind the sheep.

He saw many birds and animals on the hills. David wore a gay coloured cloak over his shoulders, and he carried a shepherd's crook in his hand.

David carried pebbles in a small bag, and he had a catapult. If a sheep went too far away, David threw a pebble. This made the sheep run back to the flock.

David sang as he led his sheep up and down the hills.

David had a small harp. Sometimes, when the sheep were safely feeding, David would sit down and make music.

David sang songs about God's beautiful world. He listened to the birds and the wind, and the sounds all around him.

The lovely things David heard and saw helped him to make his music.

Now there was a holy man named Samuel, who served God and taught the people. God told Samuel that one day David would be a king.

Samuel went to David's father and asked to see his youngest son. Then Samuel poured holy oil on David's head as a sign that God had chosen him to be His servant.

David wondered why he had been chosen. He knew that God would help him to be a good king, just as God had helped him to be a good shepherd boy.

# THE BOY JESUS

When Jesus was a little boy, He saw crowds of people going on a journey to the Temple in Jerusalem. They were going to a special service called ' The Feast of the Passover '.

Jesus wanted to go, too, but He was not old enough.

When Jesus was twelve, He was then old enough to go with Mary and Joseph to the great Temple.

It was a long way to Jerusalem. Jesus helped His mother Mary to pack food to eat on the way. Joseph got the donkey ready. He put the food in the saddle bags and fastened rugs on, too.

Then they went to join the other people from the village who were waiting to start. Friends of Jesus called, "Hurry up!" to each other. They were so excited to be going to Jerusalem at last.

On the third day after leaving home, the tired travellers saw high on the hills the walls of Jerusalem, and the shining roof of the Temple. It was a wonderful sight.

At last they came to the courts of the Temple, where wise men sat answering questions about God's Book. The men were called Rabbis— or Teachers.

Jesus wanted to ask questions and to hear more about God, so He waited there.

Jesus asked the teachers many questions, and was able to answer all those He was asked. The teachers were surprised that He knew so much about God's Book.

When Mary and Joseph started home again, they could not find Jesus anywhere. They were worried, and went back to look for Him. At last they found Jesus with the teachers.

He was surprised that Mary and Joseph had not guessed that He was in God's House. Then He went back home to Nazareth with them.

# THE BOY WHO
## HELPED JESUS

There was a boy who lived not far from the Sea of Galilee. He could play by the seaside, as well as climb the grassy hills nearby.

It was fun being out of doors. There were so many things to see and do.

One sunny day, his mother packed five little barley loaves and two small fishes for him to have a picnic on the hillside.

The boy saw a big crowd on the hillside.

"Jesus must be talking to them," said the boy to himself. He climbed fast, and soon he was sitting on the grass, close to Jesus.

When Jesus finished talking, it was late. He knew how hungry everyone must be.

" Where can we buy food ? " Jesus asked His friends.

The boy wanted to help Jesus.

" Jesus can have my lunch," said the boy to Andrew, who was a friend of Jesus.

So Andrew said to Jesus:

" There is a lad here with five barley loaves and two small fishes; but what are they among so many? "

Jesus smiled at the boy, who held out his lunch.

Then Jesus stretched out His hand and gently took the food from the boy.

The boy was so glad to help Jesus, Who held the food in His hands. Then Jesus said Grace, thanking God for what they were about to eat.

" Tell the people to sit down," said Jesus to His friends. So everyone sat down, and Jesus shared out the food.

The boy saw how Jesus made the lunch enough to share with everyone.